EVERY WORD

A dad's desire to share with his children the
importance of knowing God based on His word

STEPHEN BEECHWOOD

WESTBOW
P R E S S®
A DIVISION OF THOMAS NELSON
& ZONDERVAN

WestBow Press books may be ordered through booksellers or by contacting:

WestBow Press
A Division of Thomas Nelson & Zondervan
1663 Liberty Drive
Bloomington, IN 47403
www.westbowpress.com
1 (866) 928-1240

Unless otherwise noted, all scripture quotations are from the Good
News Translation (GNT) in Today's English Version- Second Edition
Copyright © 1992 by American Bible Society. Used by Permission.

Scripture quotations marked (NKJV) are from the New King James Version®.
Copyright © 1982 by Thomas Nelson. Used by permission. All rights reserved.

ISBN: 978-1-9736-6204-4 (sc)
ISBN: 978-1-9736-6205-1 (e)

Print information available on the last page.

WestBow Press rev. date: 6/18/2019

Contents

This book was originally going to be dedicated to Ashley, Adam and Courtney. However, because organizing my notes has spanned several decades, it is now also dedicated to their spouses, Michael, Jen and Aaron, their children and, if the Lord tarries, their children and grandchildren.

Acknowledgments

Many thanks to Adam for making the time and taking the time to edit each chapter of this book. His attention to detail found typos that the spell-checker missed and his recommended rewordings brought the clarity I had intended.

Preface

There is no end to the writing of books, and too much study will wear you out. After all this, there is only one thing to say: Have reverence for God, and obey His commands, because this is all that we were created for. (Ecclesiastes 12:12-13)

If there is no end to the writing of books and too much study will wear you out, why am I writing this book? Primarily because my experience has been that there are not too many people who are reading the one book from which to learn reverence for God, i.e., the Bible. For years, whenever someone mentions that they are in a book club, I ask them if the club has ever read the Bible or, since "Bible" means "books", if the club has ever read one of the books of the Bible, e.g., The Gospel According to Mark. The answer to both questions is always, "No." So, if people are reading other books, perhaps they will read this book and then consider reading God's books found in the Bible. My assumption is that you already have a favorite author and desire to read everything she or he has written. My hope is that by reading this book, you will discover a new favorite Author and want to read all His books.

1

A Perfect World

Jesus didn't come to make bad people good; He
came to make spiritually dead people alive! [1]

A perfect world

Several years ago, on a warm summer afternoon, several
friends (couples) joined Susan and me in the gazebo in our
backyard. As we sat around the table in the center of the
gazebo, someone shared some information about a friend.
The reaction to "the news" spanned the full spectrum from
some who said, "I already knew" to shock, disbelief and
denial among the rest of us. The conversation continued
for several minutes with each person weighing in with their
opinion about the situation. Someone then made a summary
statement: "We don't live in a perfect world." Everyone
agreed. Then someone said, "Hey Stephen, why didn't God
create a perfect world?" I didn't hesitate. I said, "He did! In the
Garden of Eden!" That answer drew a unanimous response,
"Don't go there! Let's not have that conversation! Let's not

ruin the afternoon!" I acquiesced and the conversation went in another direction.

The truth remains: God originally *did* create a perfect world and, in creating Adam and Eve, he created a perfect couple, each with a mind, body, soul and their human nature. God also gave them a living *spirit* by which they would commune with Him through His Holy Spirit. A simple picture of this relationship looks like this:

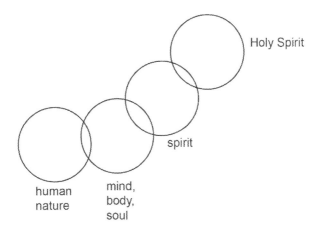

But something went terribly wrong. When Adam and Eve disobeyed God and ate of the "forbidden" fruit *(Genesis 2:15-17; 3:1-7)*, they died – not physically but *spiritually.* Their way of communing with God was gone. The updated picture of this new relationship looks like this:

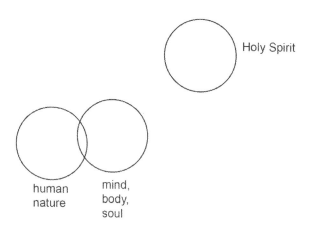

And because we are all descendants of Adam and Eve, the picture above also shows our relationship with God when we are born. We are all born *spiritually dead*. What does it mean to be born spiritually dead? It means that your physical life begins with no knowledge of God, no understanding of God and, as you grow up, you have little or no interest in learning about God. You probably weren't even aware that an important part of you, your *spirit*, is missing. Your *spirit* is what Jesus was talking about when he said, *"You must be born again" (John 3:3-7).* He was announcing that if you want to restore your relationship with God, the part of you that is missing *must* be replaced with a new spirit.

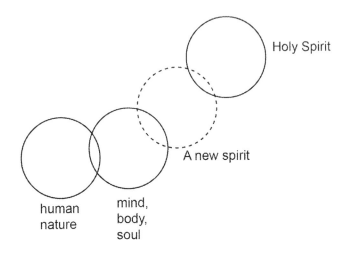

An important distinction

You may be thinking, "I thought I already have a spirit. Isn't that what my soul is?" Not according to the Bible. According to the Bible, your *soul* and *spirit* are separate and distinct *(1Thessalonians 5:23)*.

Your soul

Every person is born with a *soul*. Your soul is that part of you that has no physical reality but is associated with everything about you that is alive, i.e., your thoughts, emotions, intellect, understanding, conscience, and your ability to reason, make decisions and make choices. What's more, your *soul* is immortal. Your *soul* will live on after your body breathes its final breath. Your *soul* is what needs to be restored to a right relationship with God *(1Peter 1:6-9)*.

You may be asking, "If it is my *soul* that needs to be restored, why is *spirit* the missing circle?" The answer is that your *soul* cannot discern the things of God without a new *spirit* (*1Corinthians 2:14*). You soul needs a *spirit* to understand the things of God.

Your spirit

What, then, is your *spirit*? Like most words, the word *spirit* can mean many things depending on the context in which it is used. For example, following are a few of more than 20 definitions you will find in a dictionary:

- pride or enthusiasm, as in *the students have school spirit*
- a pleasant demeanor, as in *she has a gentle spirit*
- feelings or mood, as in *he has a troubled spirit*

You can probably identify with those definitions and many of the other definitions found in a dictionary. Those definitions (and many others found in the dictionary) also appear in context in the Bible. However, there is one more definition of *spirit* that appears in the Bible that *does not* appear in dictionaries. Within the Bible, you learn that your *spirit* is: *a new person, a new creation (2Corinthians 5:17), <u>the new you</u> that is born again through the Holy Spirit.*

An extremely important truth

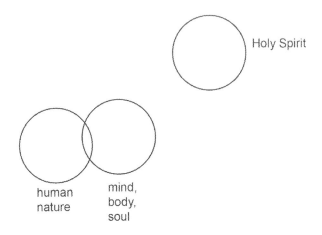

The left side of the diagram (your human nature and your mind, body and soul) represents all who have been born naturally (physically), who have not yet been born spiritually (per the definition above). The left side of the diagram also represents an extremely important truth found in the Bible and that is, a person born naturally *cannot* understand the spiritual things of God *(1Corinthians 2:14)*. There is a gap in their understanding. Not only do they not understand the spiritual things of God, they actually consider those things *foolishness (1Corinthians 1:25)*.

A *foolish* example

Consider the following verse from the Bible: *Someone who is always thinking about happiness is a fool. A wise person thinks about death. (Ecclesiastes 7:4)*. A paraphrase in today's English would read, *It is better to go to a wake or a funeral than to a party*. Over the years, when I have quoted that verse and/or the paraphrase, I have heard a variety of responses:

- "That's ridiculous!"
- "That doesn't make sense."
- "That's crazy!"
- "That's stupid!"
- "Right! (*sarcastically*) Everyone knows it's more fun to go to a funeral than to a party!"

My favorite response is, "That's stupid!" The reason it's my favorite is because "stupid" is a synonym for *foolish* or *foolishness* and there's a verse in the Bible that says, *God's foolishness is wiser than men (1Corinthians 1:25).* The natural person dismisses the verse as foolishness. The new person (the one who has been given their new spirit as defined above) is able to discern the wisdom in a verse that says it's better to go to a wake or funeral than to a party. Discernment comes after recognizing the importance of reading your Bible.

---

1   *Ravi Zacharias on Twitter: https://twitter.com/ravizacharias/ status/ 403333034134364161*

2

The Importance of Reading Your Bible

*All Scripture is inspired by God and is useful for
teaching the truth, rebuking error, correcting faults, and
giving instruction for right living. (2Timothy 3:16)*

An object lesson

My assumption is that you know what a Swiss Army knife
is - not only a knife but a tool that contains many other tools.

Many years ago, I heard a children's sermon in which the
speaker held up a closed Swiss Army knife and asked the
children, "What do you think is in here?" The speaker then
began writing their guesses on a flip chart:

- a knife
- scissors
- a screw driver
- that other kind of screw driver
- a can opener
- etc.

After they ran out of guesses, the speaker slowly opened the knife to reveal each of the tools. Children and adults realized three things:

1. They were right about some of the things that were in there
2. Things they thought were in there, weren't
3. Things were in there that they hadn't thought of

The speaker then announced, "It is the same with the Bible! Unless you open it and read it,

- you will not know if you are right about what's in there
- you will think that there are things in there that aren't
- you will discover that there are things in there that you hadn't thought of."

How well do you know someone?

How well do you know someone? To help answer the question, turn it around and ask, how well does someone know *you*? The answer is: Someone knows <u>you</u> *only as well as you <u>let</u> them know you*. Returning to the original question, you will know someone *only as well as s/he lets you know them*.

The Bible is God's revelation about Himself to <u>you</u> and to the rest of the world. He already knows you better than you know yourself. What He wants is for *you* to know *Him*. Take a minute and let that fact sink in! The Creator of the universe has taken the time to put in writing what He wants you to know about Him. One of the things He wants you to know about Him is that He has your best interests in mind. Within the pages of His book you will discover, for example, instructions for right living. Some of the instructions for right living *will help you recognize wisdom and good advice, and help you understand sayings with deep meaning. They (the instructions) can teach you how to live intelligently, and how to be honest, just and fair. They can make an inexperienced person clever and teach young men how to be resourceful. They can even add to the knowledge of wise men and give guidance to the educated, so that they can understand the hidden meanings of proverbs and the problems that the wise raise. (Proverbs 1:2-6)* Not only that, God often lets you know ahead of time what the consequences of your behavior will be - regardless of whether you believe in Him.

Bragging rights

Do you find it hard to believe that God wants <u>you</u> to know <u>Him</u>? Listen to what He says: *"The wise should not boast of their wisdom, nor the strong of their strength, nor the rich of their wealth. If any want to boast, they should boast that they know and understand me, because my love is constant, and I do what is just and right. These are the things that please me. I, the Lord, have spoken." (Jeremiah 9:23-24)*

How do you get to know and understand God? By reading the Bible.

Do you have to read the whole thing? Surely you don't need to read the Old Testament, do you? A simple analogy should suffice to answer those two questions: If you received a long letter from someone who cares deeply for you, who has your best interests in mind, would you intentionally ignore half the letter?

"'Human beings cannot live on bread alone, but need every word that God speaks." (Matthew 4:4)

Every word

Every word?! Yes! At the *detail* level, "every" means *each* word read in historical, literary context. At the *summary* level, "every" means the entire Bible. Why do you need every word? The following example should help answer that question:

Let's assume you enjoy reading history and someone mentions that the book of Acts (the fifth book in the New Testament) is the history of the early church following the resurrection of Jesus. Based on that information you decide to read Acts first. (Note: you may be asking yourself, *Why would someone start reading the Bible in the middle?* Recalling that "Bible" means "books", you could put each book of the Bible in its own binding and then line the books up on a bookshelf in the same sequence as they appear in the Bible. Each book stands on its own. You may begin reading any one of them first.) After reading Acts, if someone asked you, "Who raised Jesus from death" you would answer, "God!" because you read in Acts 4:8-10 ... *Jesus Christ of Nazareth—whom you crucified and whom God raised from death.* You would know that *detail* from that verse. If Acts was the only book you ever read, you would miss the following *details* found elsewhere in the Bible:

- *... and God the Father, who raised him (Jesus) from death. (Galatians 1:1)*
- *Jesus answered, "Tear down this Temple, and in three days I will build it again." (John 2:19-22)*

- *If the Spirit of God, who raised Jesus from death, lives in you, then he who raised Christ from death will also give life to your mortal bodies by the presence of his Spirit in you. (Romans 8:11)*

By reading the entire Bible - the *summary* level - you learn that Jesus was raised from death by God, i.e., *God the Father, God the Son,* and *God the Holy Spirit.* This is not a *contradiction;* this is a *revelation* that God wants you to know about Him. He (one God) exists as three persons.

Job One

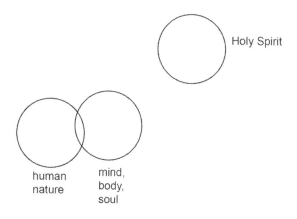

In the opening chapter, you learned an extremely important truth found in the Bible: a person born naturally *cannot* understand the spiritual things of God, that there is a gap in their understanding. If everyone is born spiritually dead, how does that gap get closed? If you start reading the Bible, how can you possibly understand what the Bible says if that gap is there? Closing the gap is "Job One" for the Holy Spirit.

The Holy Spirit is constantly tugging, poking, pushing, and prodding you through people, places and events to make you realize that there is a God, that He is real, that He is closer than the air you breath and never further away than your stiff outstretched arm.

Getting started

Have you ever needed a sponge and when you looked for one under the kitchen sink, the one you found was bone-dry and hard-as-a-rock as if it had been out in the desert during an extended drought? Have you ever paid close attention to what happens when you put that sponge under the faucet and turn the water on to get the sponge wet? The initial flow of water actually bounces off the sponge! When you begin reading the Bible you may have a similar experience, i.e., the words of the Bible may simply bounce off you. The best way to prevent that from happening is to pray a simple prayer each time you pick up the Bible to read it, e.g., Heavenly Father, please open my eyes to see the truth in Your word, open my ears to hear it, and refresh my mind that with the help of Your Spirit I may understand it, retain it, recall it, and put it into practice. I ask this in the name of Your Son Jesus. Amen.

Following are five recommendations to help you get started reading the Bible.

1. **Start reading**
    -   Set aside time each day to read the Bible. Someone figured out that if you read a red-letter version of the Bible, i.e., one in which the words of Jesus appear as **red text**, you can read

everything Jesus said in 4 *hours* - not four years, not four months, not four weeks, not four days but four *hours*.

- There is no bad place to begin reading the Bible, but some places are better than others. I once heard someone say that if you only read one book of the Bible, read the Gospel according to Mark.
- Use commentaries that are available to the public via online resources such as BibleStudyTools.com
- Find a mentor who can help explain what you're reading.

2. **Study the Bible**.
   - Take notes when you're reading so that you will see the consistency across other books.
   - Attend a Bible study.
   - Listen to Bible studies on tape, CD, or other electronic devices.

3. **Put what you read into practice**.
   - *Do not deceive yourselves by just listening to his word; instead, put it into practice. (James 1:22)*

4. **Listen to someone who preaches what the Bible says**.
   - Preachers who preach verse-by-verse through an entire book of the Bible.
   - Preachers who preach on a topic, drawing from all parts of the Bible regarding that topic.
   - Listen to preachers in church, on the radio, online, on recordings, etc.

5. **Memorize portions of what you read that resonate with you**.

   - Memorizing (not required, but highly recommended) helps you remember the right things to put into practice. *I keep your law in my heart, so that I will not sin against you. (Psalm 119:11)*

As you do *one, some,* or *all* of the recommendations above, don't stop reading when you encounter some of those churchy words like *sin* and *repent*.

3

Those "churchy" words

Sin speaks to the wicked deep in their hearts; they reject God and do not have reverence for him. Because they think so highly of themselves, they think that God will not discover their sin and condemn it. (Psalm 36:1-2)

From that time Jesus began to preach his message: "Repent, because the kingdom of heaven is near!" (Matthew 4:17)

If you had to reduce the Bible to just one word

At an evening Bible study, I once heard the facilitator ask the participants, "If you had to reduce the Bible to just one word, what would that word be?" The facilitator then handed everyone a piece of paper, asked them to write their answer on the paper, fold it in half, and hand the paper back to him. After everyone had written their answer and handed it to the facilitator, the facilitator opened the first piece of paper, read the word aloud, and asked the owner to explain why s/he chose that word. There were 10 participants that evening. There were 10 different answers!

1. *Love*
2. *God*
3. *Jesus*
4. *Truth*
5. *Faith*
6. *Forgiveness*
7. *Holy Spirit*
8. *Hope*
9. *Resurrection*

As each person explained the reason for their choice, the others nodded in agreement, acknowledging that they understood why the person chose their particular word. The 10th answer surprised everyone. The 10th answer was *Sin*. The person who wrote *Sin* explained that if Adam and Eve hadn't sinned (or any of their descendants), there would never have been a need to write the Bible. Good point!

But the truth is, we're all sinners and our sin separates us from God. Adam and Eve's sin in the Garden caused the gap that separates us from God. What's more, God tells us that we are sinners:

- by nature *(Romans 5:12)*
- by choice *(Psalm 14:1-3; Romans 1:21)*
- by divine decree *(Romans 3:9-18,23)*

God tells us that we have all inherited a sinful nature from Adam and Eve. That sinful nature permeates our souls to a level lower than our genes and DNA. The great preacher Charles Hayden Spurgeon summed up this reality when he said: "As the salt flavors every drop in the Atlantic, so does sin affect every atom of our nature. It is so sadly there, so abundantly there, that if you cannot detect it, you are deceived."

You may be thinking, "Sin is such a churchy word. No one talks about sin anymore. Shouldn't the discussion be about good behavior and bad behavior? As long as the good outweighs the bad, and as long as we love one another, isn't that what matters? Do we really need to talk about sin?"

Yes! A thousand times, yes! When people avoid talking about sin and instead talk in generalities about making sure the good in their life outweighs the bad, and that love is all that matters, they are making the same mistake that Adam and Eve made. They are choosing their own *reasoning* and *rationalization* over God's *revelation* (we are sinners by nature, by choice and by divine decree) and sin _must_ be addressed before you die if you are to be restored to a right relationship with God. If you reject the idea of sin … or believe you have no sin … or believe you have not sinned … or choose to ignore or redefine what God calls sin, you deceive yourself. *(1John 1:8-10)* You are choosing your own *reasoning* and *rationalization* over God's *revelation*.

Job One revisited

An earlier chapter stated that "Job One" of the Holy Spirit is to raise your *sense of awareness* about the way you view the world. A more detailed description of Job One includes (but is not limited to) *proving to the people of the world that they are wrong about sin and about what is right and about God's judgment. (John 16:8)* What should be your response to that revelation?

As you read your Bible you will learn (at the detail level and the summary level) where your understanding about God (or Jesus or the Bible) is wrong and where your behavior is in opposition to God's word. When that happens, God grants you the opportunity to repent.

John the Baptizer (whose role was to prepare people for the coming of Jesus) preached a message of repentance coupled with a sense of urgency, *"Turn away from your sins," he said, "because the Kingdom of heaven is near!"* (*Mark 1:4*) After John was arrested and put in prison for confronting Herod (the ruler of Galilee) about Herod's sin *(Mark 6:18-19),* Jesus began his own public ministry with the exact same message and same sense of urgency, "The right time has come," he said, "and the Kingdom of God is near! Turn away from your sins and believe the Good News!" *(Mark 1:15)*

Why the sense of urgency? It's not *urgency* as much as it is *opportunity.* The *opportunity* to repent is near (available) right now! Have you seized the opportunity or are you letting the opportunity pass by? Are you rationalizing your delay because you think, "*God would never take me the way I am* <u>or</u> *you don't know the things I've done in my life* <u>or</u> *let me have some time to clean up my life a bit and then I will be able to repent.*" God does not require you to clean up your life one iota before you repent. That's grace! He takes you just as you are whenever and wherever you are on the spectrum of your life and will begin a new work in you.

Finally, repentance does not simply mean feeling sorry over sin each time you commit it. Genuine repentance goes beyond feeling sorry and includes the emotional elements of sincere regret and remorse along with *changing your mind* about sin, about what's right and wrong and about God's judgment. It includes a life-long desire to replace your sinful behavior with obedience to God. Your life-long desire is in response to God's love - for allowing Himself to be nailed to a cross so that you might be restored to a right relationship with Him. *Might* be restored? God grants you the *opportunity* to repent. He doesn't *force* you to *respond to His grace.* His hope is that you will believe Him, put your faith in Him, and trust Him. *What will be your response?*

4

That "churchy" statement

"You must be born again." (John 3:3-7)

"You must be born again."

What's your reaction to that statement? Is your reaction one or more of the following?

- *I don't like it.*
- *I don't like hearing it*
- *I don't like being told that I must be born again.*
- *I don't like listening to people who want to tell me that they're born again.*
- *I don't like being around people who talk that way.*
- *I get embarrassed when I'm around people who talk that way.*
- *That saying is too churchy for me.*

Can you identify with one or more of the reactions listed above? Do you have another reaction? Have you ever stopped to ask yourself why you react the way you do to that statement?

Why do those words cause such an adverse reaction in so many people? Consider the following explanation: when you hear those words, "You must be born again," your *human nature* triggers the "fight or flight" response. Your human nature can't remain neutral because it is threatened by an alternate way of living. Your human nature knows that if you receive a new spirit, you might begin making choices based on what your spirit wants, not on what your human nature wants. What your *human nature* wants is contrary to what your *spirit* wants; what your spirit wants is contrary to what your human nature wants. *(Galatians 5:17)* Referring back to the diagram,

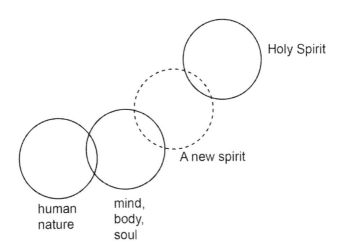

notice that *there is no overlap* of your human nature and your new spirit. There are no common denominators between your human nature and your new spirit.

A loophole?

As the story goes, one time when American comedian, actor, juggler, and writer W.C. Fields was sick in bed, his friend came into his room to see how he was feeling. Knowing that he was an avowed non-believer he was surprised to see him sitting up in bed reading the Bible. He asked him, "What are you doing?" He answered, "I'm looking for a loophole."

Jesus said, "*You must be born again.*" (*John 3:3-7*) Despite that, are you still hopeful that if you don't go along with being "born again" *before* you die that God will provide another way for you to be restored to a right relationship with Him *after* you die? Are you hoping, like *W.C. Fields*, there's a loophole for you and others who don't want to be "born again" right now? You might want to consider what Jesus had to say about that:

> *If people hear my message and do not obey it,*
> *I will not judge them. I came, not to judge the*
> *world, but to save it. Those who reject me and*
> *do not accept my message have one who will*
> *judge them. The words I have spoken will be*
> *their judge on the last day!* (*John 12:47-48*)

There is no loophole. Read it again:

> *Those who reject me and do not accept my*
> *message have one who will judge them. The*
> *words I have spoken will be their judge on the*
> *last day!*

You *must* be born again. You may be saying, "That's not fair!" But it is. Think of it like a game. God has announced to you and the rest of the world up front, in the Bible (His rule book), what the stakes are to be restored to a right relationship with Him: "You *must* be born again." What *wouldn't* be fair is if God waited until *after* you died to tell you that you should have been able to figure out on your own that *you must be born again.*

You may be thinking, "Well Jesus said that 'He didn't come to *judge* the world but to *save* the world.' I'm part of the world, doesn't that mean I'm already saved?" No. The Bible teaches that the people who have been saved are those who have been *born again.* (*John 1:12*) What's more, they are also called children of God. "Aren't we all children of God?" No. The Bible teaches that we are all *creations* of God. (*Psalm 139:13*) He knew ahead of time that you would be *you*, i.e., your sex, how tall you would be, the color of your hair, the color of your eyes, the shape of your nose, the number of days allotted to you for your life, etc. He knew because the Bible teaches that He made all those decisions about you. You *become* a child of God when you are born again. When you are born again, you are *adopted* into the family of God as one of His children. (*Ephesians 1:5*)

You are "born again" when you receive your new spirit from the Holy Spirit, the topic of discussion after we talk next about your human nature.

5

Your human nature

Those who obey their human nature
cannot please God. (Romans 8:8)

Well-rounded

If you go through life without an understanding of God *based on His Word*, your life lessons come from your surroundings. You form your opinions, make decisions, say and do things based on your upbringing, your family, friends, co-workers, neighbors, education, personal experiences, experiences of others, the books-magazines-periodicals you read, news stations you listen to, the latest poll results, information on the Internet, etc. As well-rounded as information from so many sources might appear, the Bible refers to that existence (all that information but no knowledge of God and no understanding of God based on His word) as *living in darkness. (Ephesians 4:17-19)*

Total eclipse

In a total solar eclipse, the moon travels slowly across the face of the sun. As it does, it blocks the light of the sun and the earth grows darker and darker. When the moon completely covers the sun (totally eclipses the sun), the earth is left in darkness.

Returning to the original diagram of one's human nature and mind, body and soul, if you were to merge the two circles into one circle - similar to the way the moon and sun are merged into one circle during an eclipse - the analogy is another total eclipse, i.e., a self-centered existence living in *spiritual darkness*.

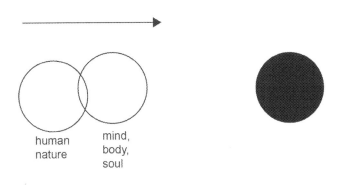

human
nature

mind,
body,
soul

Someone may object, "I'm not a religious person but I believe in Jesus. I believe he was a real person who lived 2,000 years ago. Surely you're not saying I'm living in darkness?" If you simply believe that Jesus was a real person who lived 2,000 years ago, that's a *history* lesson. If you have no other knowledge of Him *based on His word*, yes, you are living in *spiritual darkness*.

Someone else may object, "I'm not a religious person either but I believe Jesus was God's son. Surely you're not saying I'm living in darkness?" If you simply parrot at baptisms, Christmas, Easter, weddings and funerals that Jesus was God's son, that's a *theology* lesson. If you have no other knowledge of Him *based on His Word*, yes, you are living in *spiritual darkness*.

And you will continue to live in spiritual darkness until you begin to know God *based on His Word*. When you begin to know God *based on His Word*, your spiritual darkness will begin to lift in the same way that the first ray of sunlight re-appears at the end of a total eclipse. (*Ephesians 5:8-17*)

Is our human nature bad?

In the beginning, as God spoke creation into existence, He was pleased with what He saw. (*Genesis 1:4,10,12,18,21,25*) On the 6th day He looked at all He had created and was *very* pleased. (*Genesis 1:31*) Included in all His creation with which He was pleased was the creation of Adam and Eve and that would include their human nature. Their human nature worked in concert with their mind, body, soul, and spirit. Each component was in perfect harmony with the others, similar to the way all four singers are in harmony in a barbershop quartet. But when Adam and Eve's desire for knowledge of good and evil overpowered their desire to obey and please God, they ate of the fruit and died *spiritually*. In an instant, a member of the quartet (their spirit) died and the multi-part harmony was destroyed. In that split second, Adam and Eve began seeing, thinking, hearing, behaving and feeling what life without their spirit was like and, as is often the case with all of us, they began experiencing consequences they hadn't anticipated after they made what they thought was a good decision.

So is our human nature bad? The answer is, *not necessarily.* However, without a new spirit, you will live as your human nature tells you to. You will be finessed by, influenced by, controlled by and, at times, dominated by the *desires* of your human nature. *Finessed by, influenced by* and *dominated by* are all forms of control. Since that is true, you need to hear what God says about being controlled by your human nature: *And so people become enemies of God when they are controlled by their human nature; for they do not obey God's law, and in fact they cannot obey it. Those who obey their human nature cannot please God. (Romans 8:7-8)*

Desires

Not all desires are bad. For example, you desire water when you are thirsty; you desire sleep when you are tired; you desire to help when you learn that a friend or acquaintance is in need. Jesus had desires. For example, He said, "I have wanted so much to eat this Passover meal with you before I suffer!" (*Luke 22:15*) Herod had desires – he desired to see Jesus to see if Jesus would perform some miracles. (*Luke 23:8*) God has desires – He says that He desires that all people will turn from their sins and come to know the truth. (*2 Peter 3:9*)

Not all desires are good. For example, those associated with our senses of seeing, hearing, smelling, tasting and touching, have the potential, like a river, to overflow their natural banks and cause tremendous harm, damage, destruction and sometimes death. These days the word *lust* seems to be used only when referring to an overpowering *sexual* desire. A trip to the dictionary reveals that *lust* is defined as *an overpowering desire of <u>any</u> of the senses.*

Another example of a harmful desire is the desire to get rich. God warns that *those who want to get rich fall into temptation and are caught in the trap of many foolish and harmful desires, which pull them down to ruin and destruction.* (*1 Timothy 6:9*) Did you notice the double use of the word "desire" in what God says? A single overpowering desire can lead to poor decisions that result in getting caught in a downward spiral of many other foolish and harmful desires.

With or without a new spirit, your human nature and desires can have a very powerful influence on you.

The spectrum of good and evil

Human Nature
Thoughts and Behavior
Bad -- Good

We <u>all</u> live somewhere on the spectrum of human nature between good thoughts and bad thoughts, good behavior and bad behavior. Your position on the spectrum is not fixed, it is variable, as if on a sliding scale. Your position on the spectrum may be influenced by people, places and events and result in sliding toward "good" behavior when, for example, you respond to help people impacted by a natural disaster. Your position may slide towards bad behavior when, for example, anger boils over into verbal abuse and/or physical abuse. Unfortunately, the left hand side of the scale doesn't stop at *bad* behavior, it slithers into *evil* behavior.

One news story this evening was about a man who had been arrested months ago and admitted that he had been planning to kidnap, torture, rape, kill and cannibalize children.[1] A search of his home confirmed that he was well on his way down that path. A few people wondered if he had already implemented his plan.

A Filter

I have a friend who is thinking about writing a book on *communication*. She has been gathering real-world examples, some funny, some rude, that she will include in her book. She intends to emphasize the importance of having a filter between one's mind and one's mouth, i.e., a filter that prevents things from being blurted out; a filter that holds back statements and/or questions so that they may be re-considered, re-worded, and perhaps even suppressed, before being stated aloud.

In a similar way, our human nature also needs a filter. What is that filter? Your new spirit. Your new spirit <u>can</u> become that filter. *Using* the filter will still be a choice.

Your human nature

There are (and have been) many people in the world who do not believe in God, who do good or great things for humanity. No doubt that is true. But it doesn't change the fact that if they do those things with no knowledge of God and no understanding of God based on His word, they are doing them in spiritual darkness. The question becomes, what is their motive? They may accomplish something really great and achieve some level of satisfaction or fulfillment or accolades from the world. But whatever they accomplish, they will not achieve their salvation*. Their work, their efforts, no matter how altruistic, even if they could do them for eternity, do *nothing* to restore their relationship with God. They may have gained the world but will have forfeited their soul. (*Matthew 16:26*)

* Salvation is another one of those churchy words. Salvation means saved. Saved from what? Eternal separation from God. Saved by whom? God.

---

1   The Boston Globe, Sep 17, 2013: https://www.bostonglobe.com/metro/2013/09/17/worcester-man-who-wanted-cannibalize-children-sentenced-years-federal-prison/srAauLfHVbkjqdHUTVlglM/story.html

6

Your soul

"My soul is prepared to die. Is yours?"[1]

A statement and a question

In the movie, Indiana Jones and the Last Crusade, you learn that there is a secret organization whose main purpose is to prevent everyone (good guys and bad guys) from finding the Holy Grail, the cup Jesus drank from at the Last Supper. In one scene, a member of the secret organization is fist fighting with Indiana Jones to prevent him from obtaining information that would lead him to the Holy Grail. Their fight takes place in a rowboat that's slowly drifting towards an enormous, slowly rotating propeller of a large ship. Every couple punches, Indiana Jones looks over his shoulder to see how much closer they have drifted. Following one particular glance, after the propeller has actually started chopping off the end of their boat, the protector of the Holy Grail makes a statement and asks a question. He says, "My soul is prepared to die. Is yours?" It's a great statement and a great question! We'll come back to both.

What is your soul?

The quick answer is: your soul is that part of you that is not physical. Your soul:

- gives life to your body, i.e., is the definition of "alive"
- is your consciousness - confirming that you are aware that you exist
- is the source of your thoughts
- feels emotions
- has desires
- makes decisions
- does not die
- leaves your body at physical death and continues to live for eternity. (Luke 16:22-23)

A different perspective

Given that your soul does not die, rather than say (as most people do), "I have a soul", it is more accurate to say, "I am a soul," and the short time I am here on this earth, "I have a body". It is your soul that begins life with no knowledge of God, no understanding of God and, as you grow up, has little or no interest in learning about God. It is your soul that sins. It is your soul that needs to be restored to a right relationship with God. If you are like most people, you probably don't give much thought to your soul. Who takes time to think about something you can't see, feel or touch when you have many other "real world" things competing for your time?

A different priority

Jesus shared the following story about a man who had a To Do list who planned to get around to other things after he finished the list.

> "There was once a rich man who had land which bore good crops. He began to think to himself, 'I don't have a place to keep all my crops. What can I do? This is what I will do,' he told himself; 'I will tear down my barns and build bigger ones, where I will store the grain and all my other goods. Then I will say to myself, Lucky man! You have all the good things you need for many years. Take life easy, eat, drink, and enjoy yourself!' But God said to him, 'You fool! This very night you will have to give up your life; then who will get all these things you have kept for yourself?'" (Luke 12:16-20)

You will have to give up your life means your earthly life is at an end and the first order of new business for your soul is to give an account of your earthly life to God. The Bible tells us that *There is nothing that can be hid from God; everything in all creation is exposed and lies open before His eyes. And it is to Him that we must all give an account of ourselves. (Hebrews 4:13)* Clearly this man's soul was not prepared to die. His focus was on earthly things. His focus was on himself as evidenced by all the pronouns he used in a conversation with himself!

The protector's statement revisited

Are you ready to give an account of your life to God or, like the rich man, are you telling yourself that after you take care of all the things on your To Do list – all those things that require your day-to-day attention, then you will make time to do things like ponder your soul? If the latter, your priorities are reversed and unlike the protector of the Holy Grail, your soul is not prepared to die. Doing things on your To Do list isn't a bad thing. It's only a bad thing if your To Do list is being done at the expense of pondering the nature of your soul while it has a body and understanding what happens to your soul when it separates from your body at death. Jesus said, *"Instead, be concerned above everything else with the Kingdom of God and with what He requires of you, …" (Matthew 6:33)*

The protector's question

So, back to the question asked by the protector of the Holy Grail, "Is your soul prepared to die?" In the movie, Indiana Jones didn't answer directly but his actions implied his answer. He stopped fighting to avoid being chopped to pieces by the large propeller.

Bottom line: If you have a new spirit then your answer will always be "Yes!" regardless of your situation or circumstances.

---

1. Indiana Jones and the Last Crusade, dir. Steven Spielberg, 1989

7

Your spirit

*Jesus grew both in body and in wisdom, gaining
favor with God and people. (Luke 2:52)*

Growing up

Re-read the verse above. What a great summation of what
growing up is all about! Like Jesus, we are to grow in body
(physically) and wisdom (intellectually) and gain favor with
God (spiritually) and people (socially). Talk about needing
every word!! We appear to grow naturally in three of the
four areas (intellectually, physically and socially) but not
spiritually. Why is that? For starters, you must first be born
again before you can grow spiritually. Second, when you
receive your new spirit from the Holy Spirit, your new spirit
is not the same age as you are. Just to be clear on this very
important point, if for example you are 33 years old (as I was)
when you receive your new spirit, your new spirit is not 33
years old. It is a newborn. The Bible says that your new spirit
begins as any other newborn, i.e., as an infant or babe that

must be cared for as any other newborn. Therefore, consider the following:

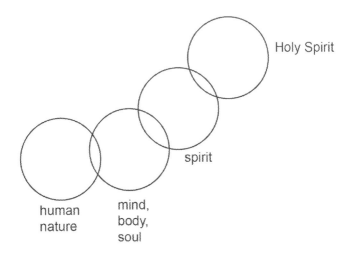

Holy Spirit

spirit

human
nature

mind,
body,
soul

The necessity of food

In the same way that a newborn needs to be fed milk, your new spirit also needs to be fed. Fed what? The Bible says spiritual milk. *(1 Peter 2:2)* What is spiritual milk? The Bible says that it is the word of God, i.e., the Bible. Regular milk provides a newborn with nourishment for sustaining physical life. The word of God provides your spirit with nourishment for sustaining spiritual life. What is the nourishment provided by spiritual milk? Truth. At the Last Supper, when Jesus prayed for Himself, His disciples and for all who will eventually believe in Him, His prayer included the following statement: *your word is truth. (John 17:17)*

Regular feedings

In the same way that newborns are fed at regular intervals, your new spirit should be fed at regular intervals. You should make/take time each day to read and study your Bible. If you are a morning person, allocate some of your early morning to spend time with God in His word. What better way to start the day than in God's word! If you are a night owl, allocate some of the end of your day to spend time with God in His word. What better way to end the day than in God's word! Regardless of when you spend time with God in His word, you (morning person) will be amazed at how often something you read will apply to a situation or conversation later in the day and something you (late-night owl) read applies to what happened during the day.

You may be thinking, "I don't have *time* to spend regular time reading the Bible!" If that is what you think, you need to be reminded about fourteen forty. 1440 is the number of minutes each one of us has in a day, no more, no less. Despite all the interesting ways we refer to time, e.g., we find time, we lose time; we save time, we spend time; we give time, we take time; we use time wisely, we waste time; etc. we each have a choice regarding how we will use our 1440 minutes. Admittedly, some of the 1440 is already ear-marked for things like sleeping, attending school, commuting, working, meal times, etc. but there are always minutes that you can reallocate. The Bible even mentions a specific activity you might want to consider reallocating time towards, i.e., time at the gym or time working out. The Bible says:

Physical exercise has some value, but spiritual exercise is valuable in every way, because it promises life for both the present and the future. (1 Timothy 4:8)

And who among us wouldn't benefit from reallocating time spent watching TV to time spent with God in His word?

Author's note: As I write this chapter, I am away from home overnight on business. It is 8 PM and I have not had dinner. My human nature is encouraging me to stop typing and go get something to eat. My spirit is encouraging me to continue typing. I'm choosing (this evening) to spend what remains of today's 1440 looking-up references to "spirit" in God's word, attempting to organize notes and thoughts about our spirit in a way that will make a difference to you the reader. Skipping a meal may not sound like a good idea nutrition-wise and may even sound like a dumb idea given that the company will pay for the meal. That's the world's perspective. However, when you stop to consider that it was food that led to Adam and Eve's fall in the Garden of Eden, intentionally skipping a meal to spend that time with God in His word is a way to honor God and draw closer to God. That's the Biblical perspective.

Solid food

In the same way that a newborn eventually needs solid food, your spirit eventually needs solid food *(1 Corinthians 3:1-2)*. What is the solid food that our spirit needs? The answer may be found in The Gospel of John, chapter 4. When Jesus and His disciples got to the well at Sychar in Samaria, we learn that Jesus' disciples went into town to buy food *(John 4:8)*.

After they returned to the well, they begged Jesus to have something to eat. But Jesus answered, *"I have food to eat that you know nothing about." So the disciples started asking among themselves, "Could somebody have brought him food?" "My food," Jesus said to them, "is to obey the will of the one who sent me and to finish the work he gave me to do. (John 4:31-34)*

Spiritual food is obeying (doing) the will of God. "Doing the will of God" is another one of those churchy statements. What does it mean? Many people think that doing the will of God means waiting for an audible voice from God or some unmistakable sign or miracle from heaven. You don't need to wait for an audible voice, a sign or a miracle. You have plenty of opportunity to do the will of God by putting what you read in the Bible into practice. *(James 1:22)* That is doing the will of God! That is what the Lord's Prayer tells us, your will be done. *(Matthew 6:10)*

What is the nourishment provided by the solid food of doing the will of God? Faith is a good answer. However, I think trust is a better answer because trust is faith in action. What's the difference? A simple example should suffice; I have all the faith in the world that God means what He says about tithing (giving Him a tenth of my gross income), *"Put Me to the test* (regarding tithing) *and you will see that I will open the windows of heaven and pour out on you in abundance all kinds of good things." (Malachi 3:10)* But do I trust Him enough to tithe? When you do the will of God and see the results of your obedience, you will be encouraged (and challenged) to trust God's will in every area of your life.

Continuing to grow

In the same way that milk and solid food will help an infant grow physically, spiritual milk and solid (spiritual) food will help you grow spiritually. *(1 Peter 2:2)* What does growing spiritually mean? It means looking at the world from God's perspective as presented to us in His word. It means understanding His plan for mankind, what pleases Him, what displeases Him, what He says at the detail level, what He says at the summary level. It means understanding the message about sin from God's perspective and why He says it is important for us to be forgiven of that sin. It means that as a spiritual babe your first words are, "I am a sinner." It means that as you continue to grow in the knowledge of God *(2 Peter 3:18)* based on His word (spiritual growth), you will gain spiritual wisdom and realize there is absolutely nothing you can say or do on your own that will restore your relationship with God such that you will eventually be able to say, "I am a sinner in need of a Savior." It means that when you reach spiritual maturity you will be able to say with the utmost confidence as the apostle Paul did, *"I am certain that nothing can separate us from his love: neither death nor life, neither angels nor other heavenly rulers or powers, neither the present nor the future, neither the world above nor the world below—there is nothing in all creation that will ever be able to separate us from the love of God which is ours through Christ Jesus our Lord."* *(Romans 8:38-39)* It means discovering a love so great that even before the world was made, God had already decided that through His Son Jesus He would provide the way for us to be restored to a right relationship with God *(Psalm 23:3)* and become His adopted children. *(Galatians 4:5)* This is grace and this is the "Good News!"

Spiritual exercise

Everyone knows that we should all participate in some form of exercise. The following quote appeared earlier in the section on Regular Feedings:

> *Physical exercise has some value, but spiritual exercise is valuable in every way, (1 Timothy 4:8)*

What is spiritual exercise? Most fitness magazines and fitness websites will tell you that walking is one of the best exercises you may do. The best definition of spiritual exercise I've seen was on a sign outside a church. The sign simply read:

EXERCISE DAILY.
WALK WITH THE LORD.

Walk with the Lord is another churchy statement. It is synonymous with doing the will of God. If the sign had been large enough, the third row probably would have advised: AND DISTANCE MATTERS LESS THAN DIRECTION.

The right way to worship

One day Jesus had a conversation with a Samaritan woman at a well. Their conversation ran along the lines of talking about different places and ways of worshipping. Here's what He had to say about the way people worship:

"But the time is coming and is already here, when by the power of God's Spirit people will worship the Father as he really is, offering him the true worship that he wants. God is Spirit, and only by the power of his Spirit can people worship him as he really is." (John 4:23-24)

What Jesus said needs to be examined carefully so we notice every word. He said,

But the time is coming	a time is coming
and is already here	and that time has arrived
when by the power of God's Spirit	when by the power of the Holy Spirit, not our power,
people will worship the Father	people will focus their worship on God, the Father,
as He really is	as the one true God
offering him the true worship	offering Him a special kind of worship, true worship
that He wants	that is acceptable to Him.

What is true worship? True worship consists of praise and thanksgiving for all that God has made known about Himself based on His word. True worship also includes our prayers which acknowledge the truth found in His word. When we worship that way, our words flow from our spirit to His Spirit, and then His Spirit expresses our words in comprehensible terms that are acceptable to the Father. *In the same way the Spirit also comes to help us, weak as we are. For we do not know how we ought to pray; the Spirit himself pleads with God for us in groans that words cannot express. (Romans 8:26)*

Based on what Jesus said to the woman at the well, and paying attention to every word, one should come to the conclusion that we need to understand all we can about our spirit so that we may know how to worship in spirit and truth. Today, far too many Christians are spiritually malnourished as a result of Biblical illiteracy. Lack of spiritual milk and spiritual food have stunted spiritual growth. And without spiritual milk and solid spiritual food, there will be no motivation or strength to do any spiritual exercise. Is it any wonder that we know so little about our spirits and how to worship in spirit and truth?

Doing God's will

One day in the future, many will say to Jesus, *'Lord, Lord! In your name we spoke God's message, by your name we drove out many demons and performed many miracles!' Then I will say to them, 'I never knew you. Get away from me, you wicked people!'* (*Matthew 7:22-23*)

What on earth did these people do that negated speaking God's message, driving out demons and performing many miracles in Jesus name? If they did all those things and Jesus still told them to get away from Him, what chance do the rest of us have who haven't done any of those three things? Actually, it's not what they did; it's what they didn't do. Then what didn't they do that would cause such a judgment from Jesus? Jesus gives us the answer. Jesus said, *"Not everyone who calls me 'Lord, Lord' will enter the kingdom of heaven, but only those who do what My Father in heaven wants them to do."* (*Matthew 7:21*) They didn't do God's will.

People are walking around today with smart phones that give them access to information about anything they want to look up. Scripture talks about the time in which we are living. *In the last days* (before Christ returns) *information will abound but people will know nothing. (Daniel 12:4, 9-10)* The statement sounds like a contradiction. How can information abound and yet people know nothing? The Internet has given everyone instant, free access to world-wide information on any topic. Information will (and already does) abound but people will know nothing about God. And if they do not know God based on His word, they will not know "what My Father in heaven wants them to do." Is it any wonder Scripture says, *"Go in through the narrow gate, because the gate to hell is wide and the road that leads to it is easy, and there are many who travel it. But the gate to life is narrow and the way that leads to it is hard, and there are few people who find it." (Matthew 7:13-14)*

8

Your heart

*I keep your law in my heart, so that I will
not sin against you. (Psalm 119:11)*

heart

The word heart appears more than 300 times in the Bible. In
the same way that the word spirit has many meanings, heart
also has many meanings. One is the obvious one, i.e., it's the
organ or muscle in your chest. For example: *The storm makes
my heart beat wildly. (Job 37:1)* However, there are only a
handful of times when the Bible refers to someone's heart in
that context. By far, the most common use of the word heart
appears to be in reference to one's mind.

Consider the words of the preacher in Ecclesiastes when he
talks about my (his own) heart. The following Scripture is
taken from the New King James Version (NKJV). Copyright
© 1982 by Thomas Nelson, Inc. Used by permission. All
rights reserved."

And I set my heart to know wisdom and to know madness and folly. (Ecclesiastes 1:17a (NKJV))

Using mind as a synonym for heart brings more clarity to the verse: And I set my mind to know wisdom and to know madness and folly. Setting one's mind means resolving to do something or focusing on something or concentrating on something. Following are a few more sayings of the preacher and their nuances for mind.

- *I communed with my heart, saying, "Look, I have gained greatness, and have gained more wisdom than all who were before me in Jerusalem. (Ecclesiastes 1:16a (NKJV)).* Stated otherwise: I pondered in my mind.
- *My heart has understood great wisdom and knowledge. (Ecclesiastes 1:16b (NKJV)).* Stated otherwise: My mind has understood.
- *I said in my heart, " Come now, I will test you with mirth; therefore enjoy pleasure"; but surely, this also was vanity (Ecclesiastes 2:1 (NKJV)).* Stated otherwise: I said in my mind; I said to myself; I told myself; I thought to myself.
- *I searched in my heart how to gratify my flesh with wine, while guiding my heart with wisdom, and how to lay hold on folly, till I might see what was good for the sons of men to do under heaven all the days of their lives. (Ecclesiastes 2:3 (NKJV)).* Stated otherwise: I searched in my mind; I looked into; I researched; I investigated; while guiding my mind with wisdom; while maintaining clarity of thought not under the influence of the wine.

- *Whatever my eyes desired I did not keep from them. I did not withhold my heart from any pleasure, for my heart rejoiced in all my labor; And this was my reward from all my labor. (Ecclesiastes 2:10 (NKJV)).* Stated otherwise: I didn't limit my mind from considering any kind of pleasure. My mind rejoiced in the result of all my labor; I celebrated in my mind all that I had accomplished.

- *Therefore, I turned my heart and despaired of all the labor in which I had toiled under the sun (Ecclesiastes 2:20 (NKJV)).* Stated otherwise: I reconsidered; I changed my mind; I changed my way of thinking; I changed my perspective.

Hope

Sometimes heart is used as a synonym for hope. *Then He spoke a parable to them, that men always ought to pray and not lose heart, (Luke 18:1 (NKJV))*

The Natural Heart

The Bible has a lot to say about the natural heart, i.e., the mind that has no knowledge of God and no understanding of God based on His word. *Then the Lord saw that the wickedness of man was great in the earth, and that every intent of the thoughts of his heart was only evil continually. (Genesis 6:5 (NKJV))*

A New Heart

The Bible talks about God giving us a new heart. *Cast away from you all the transgressions which you have committed, and get yourselves a new heart and a new spirit. (Ezekiel 18:31a (NKJV))*

Bottom line

As you read the Bible, when you encounter the word heart (as in the opening verse in this chapter), begin with the assumption that it is referring to one's mind unless the context dictates otherwise. Doing so will bring clarity to what you are reading and will reveal how important your mind is in the relationship between your soul and spirit.

9

Your new battle

Be careful how you think; your life is shaped
by your thoughts. (Proverbs 4:23)

The previous chapters introduced you to your spiritual <u>welfare</u>. This chapter introduces you to your spiritual <u>warfare</u>. This chapter is written with the assumption that you have been born again and have your new spirit. If you haven't been born again, much of this chapter will sound foolish to you.

The Battleground

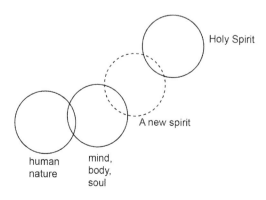

Your human nature is on one side with all its desires, your new spirit is on the other side with its desires. Your mind is the battleground in the middle that will be involved in which side wins the next battle.

> *For what our human nature wants is opposed to what the Spirit wants, and what the Spirit wants is opposed to what our human nature wants. These two are enemies, and this means you cannot do what you want to do. (Galatians 5:17)*

Activate the mechanism

In the movie For Love of the Game, while standing on the pitcher's mound and before throwing his first pitch, Billy Holiday (Kevin Costner) needed to block out the sound of the raucous fans - in Yankee Stadium no less - so he said to himself, "Activate the mechanism."[1] It was his way of making all the noise of the fans fade into the background so he could focus on what he had come to do, i.e., pitch. In the same way, as a new or veteran Christian, we all need help resisting or blocking out the noise of what our human nature wants us to say or do. We all need help, for example, when someone says something that is hurtful and our human nature wants us to respond in the same way – and in a way that leaves us feeling that we have one-upped them and gained an advantage in the situation.

How do we deal with the plethora of other situations we encounter? Each time you are faced with making a decision, you have a choice. You can make a choice based on the desire(s) of your human nature or you can make a choice based on the desire(s) of the Holy Spirit through your spirit. This implies several things:

1. If you don't have a new spirit, if you haven't been born again, your decisions will go with the flow of what your human nature wants. The possibility exists that your conscience may kick-in to consider the consequences of your decision but, in the end, you'll still be choosing something your human nature wants. And (repeating what was stated above), what your human nature wants is opposed to what the Spirit wants.

2. When you have a new spirit, your mind can still rush to a decision and make choices without considering choices available from the Holy Spirit through your spirit. When you are on automatic pilot and make decisions without the Holy Spirit, when the thought doesn't even occur to you that you could/should include the Holy Spirit in your decision, you are behaving as if you don't have a spirit. When you have a new spirit and still rush to a decision without considering choices available from the Holy Spirit, the Bible says you *quench the Spirit (1 Thessalonians 5:19 (NKJV))*, i.e., you extinguish, put out, exclude any involvement of the Spirit. When you exclude the Spirit from your decisions, the problems and cares of the world creep in and distract you from considering what the Holy Spirit wants. The good news is that the Bible uses the present tense for quench. The Bible doesn't use the past tense, you quenched the Spirit, which would make one think/believe/wonder/worry

if they had blown the one and only opportunity they would ever have of including the Holy Spirit in their decisions.

3. When you have a new spirit, your mind has the opportunity to put the brakes on your human nature's rush to a decision. Your mind has the opportunity to "activate the mechanism" and first consider what the Spirit wants vs. what your human nature wants. You then choose to either do what your human nature wants or what the Spirit wants. In these situations, if/when you still choose the way of your human nature, you do what is known as *grieve the Spirit (Ephesians 4:30 (NKJV))*. The Spirit is grieved because you considered doing what God wants you to do (put His word into practice) but you still chose to do what your human nature wants.

4. When you have a new spirit, your mind has the opportunity to choose what the Spirit wants with or without considering what your human nature wants. The Spirit recalls God's word from your memory *(John 14:26)* and passes it along to your spirit and then your mind can act accordingly. When that happens, you have truly "activated the mechanism" and you will be able to paint your human nature into a corner ... at least until the paint dries!
    In a manner of speaking, it would appear that Jesus, as man, never had an original thought, only totally obedient thoughts, because He relied on the Spirit to tell Him everything the Father wanted Jesus to say and do.

This is true, because I have not spoken on my own authority, but the Father who sent me has commanded me what I must say and speak. And I know that his command brings eternal life. What I say, then, is what the Father has told me to say." (John 12:49-50)

In an earlier chapter, the statement was made that there is no overlap between the desires of your human nature and your new spirit. *(Galatians 5:17a)* The Bible goes even further and announces that these two are enemies. *(Galatians 5:17b)* As in any conflict where there are enemies, one side wants to rule the other. The Bible says that ... *sin is crouching at your door. It wants to rule you, but you must overcome it.* The quote may be found all the way back in Genesis 4:7. God was speaking to Cain who was jealous of his brother Abel. Unfortunately, Cain was controlled by his human nature on that occasion because he ignored God's warning and murdered his younger brother. *(Genesis 4:8)* What a testimony to the power of sin in our human nature that it would have that kind of impact in the first generation of the first family!

The battle plan

So how do you "activate the mechanism" to prevent your first response being that which your human nature wants? What must you do so you may choose to respond a different way? What can you do to paint your human nature into a corner to prevent you from doing the wrong thing so that you may do the right thing by responding to the prompting of the Holy Spirit? You must ARM yourself:

Ask God to bring to remembrance His words (another job of the Holy Spirit *(John 14:26)*) so that you may respond to a situation the way He wants, not the way your human nature wants.

Remind yourself that no desire can master you unless you allow it to. Also remind yourself that a desire will master you if you try to resist it only in your own strength. You must rely on the Spirit's strength. *(Zechariah 4:6)*

Make up your mind ahead of time to do God's will no matter what the consequences.

The battle plan in action

Read the story of Joseph and Potiphar's wife *(Genesis 39)* for an example of the steps in action when properly armed.

Read the story of David and Bathsheba *(2Samuel 11)* to see what happens when one is not properly armed. One can't help but think that David quenched the Spirit throughout the entire ordeal.

Read the Temptation of Jesus *(Matthew 4:1-11)* for an example of Jesus "activating the mechanism" and being properly armed.

Final note

Jesus knew how to paint His human nature into a corner. However, even He had to deal with a human nature that was contrary to His spirit. The night before He was crucified,

He prayed in the garden of Gethsemane, *"My Father, if it is possible, take this cup of suffering from Me!"* ... but His spirit prevailed, *"Yet not what I want, but what You want." (Matthew 26:39)* Thy will be done! And a matter of hours later, Jesus said His final words, *"Jesus cried out in a loud voice, "Father! In your hands I place my spirit!" He said this and died." (Luke 23:46)* Yes, Jesus as man, had a spirit (lowercase "s") like ours.

---

1   For Love of the Game, dir. Sam Raimi, 1999

10

Trust

*Trust in the Lord with all your heart. Never rely on what
you think you know. Remember the Lord in everything
you do, and He will show you the right way. Never let
yourself think that you are wiser than you are; Simply
obey the Lord and refuse to do wrong. (Proverbs 3:5-8)*

Back to the garden

Many years ago I read the following words in one of Matthew
Henry's on-line commentaries. I have no idea which one. I
consider it the best explanation for why there is so much pain,
suffering, turmoil, and sometimes chaos, in so many personal
lives, personal relationships, and the world in general.

> *Mankind's fall began with a desire for knowledge.
> Mankind's condition persists through ignorance.*

Mankind's fall began with a desire for knowledge

Back in the Garden of Eden, God told Adam not to eat of the fruit of the tree that gives knowledge of what is good and what is evil, because if he did, he would die that same day ... *But Eve saw how beautiful the tree was and how good its fruit would be to eat and how wonderful it would be to become wise. So Eve ate the fruit and gave some to her husband and he also ate it. As soon as they had eaten it, they were given understanding ... (Genesis 3:6-7)*

Their desire for knowledge, their desire to become wise, became stronger than their desire to obey God. They could have told the serpent, "Go away!" They could have walked away themselves. They could have waited until evening when they would be walking with God in the garden *(Genesis 3:8)* to tell Him what the serpent said and ask Him if what the serpent said was true. But they didn't. Instead, they liked the sound of someone else's opinion/advice more than they valued God's revelation. They chose their own reasoning and rationalization over God's revelation and acted on their desire. And the immediate consequence of taking their first bite was that they died immediately just as God had warned, not physically but spiritually.

Mankind's condition persists through ignorance

Ignorance of what? Ignorance of what the Bible says. The message of the Bible is God's plan to show you how to be restored to a right relationship with Him, the kind of relationship that Adam and Eve enjoyed with Him in the garden before they chose their reasoning and rationalization over His revelation.

So, what's the reason you don't read the Bible? Is it because you believe the Bible is:

- old?
- antiquated?
- out of date?
- no longer relevant?
- full of contradictions?
- a bunch of myths?
- based on myths from other cultures?
- written by people who were superstitious?
- written by people with political agendas?
- not the Word of God as many people claim?
- not the Word of God as the Bible claims?
- foolishness?

If you have judged the Bible using any of these reasons, here's a reminder about His book, the word of God: *The word of God is alive and active, sharper than any double-edged sword. It cuts all the way through, to where soul and spirit meet, to where joints and marrow come together. It judges the desires and thoughts of man's heart. (Hebrews 4:12)*

It judges the desires and thoughts of your heart! All the while you may have been judging the Bible, ignoring it because you think it is old, antiquated, out of date, etc., the Bible has been judging your desires and thoughts!

Instead of judging the Bible, you should be trusting it.

Can you really trust the Bible?

Yes! One of the ways you will be convinced that you can trust the Bible, that it is the *divinely inspired* Word of God *(2 Timothy 3:16)*, that it is the *inerrant* Word of God *(John 17:17)*, that it is still *relevant (Hebrews 4:12)*, is by being attentive to the prophecies that appear within its pages. God "volunteered" men (prophets) and women (prophetesses) from all walks of life to deliver His messages. Sometimes the messages were straight-forward warnings about sinful behavior and what the consequences would be if they did not change their ways; sometimes the messages predicted a near-term fulfillment and/or a long-term fulfillment. Several hundred prophecies were about the Messiah, i.e., the promised deliverer of the Jewish nation. Following is a short list of events in the life of Jesus that are told at Christmas, Palm Sunday, the week leading up to Easter, and Easter. The list shows the Old Testament prophecy and its fulfillment in the person of Jesus of Nazareth.

Signal event	Prophesied	Fulfilled
He would be a descendant of David	Jeremiah 23:5	Matthew 1:1
He would be born in Bethlehem	Micah 5:2	Matthew 2:1
He would have a forerunner (John the Baptist)	Isaiah 40:3-4	John 1:19-23
His ministry would begin in Galilee	Isaiah 9:1	Matthew 4:12-14

Signal event	Prophesied	Fulfilled
He would ride into Jerusalem on a donkey	Zech. 9:9	Matthew 21:6-9
He would be betrayed by a friend for 30 pieces of silver	Zech. 11:12-13	Matthew 26:14-15
He would be crucified	Psalms 22:16	John 19:1-18
He would be buried in a rich man's grave	Isaiah 53:9	Matthew 27:57-60
He would rise from the dead	Psalms 16	John 20:9
His death would be the propitiation for our sins	Daniel 9:24	1 John 4:9-10 (NKJV)
He would ascend to heaven	Psalms 110:1	Acts 1:1-9
He will come again!	Acts 1:10	

Not only were all the prophecies very specific, they were also foretold hundreds of years before Jesus was born per the following table..

Prophet	Their time as prophet
Micah	740 BC
Isaiah	740-680 BC
Jeremiah	626-580 BC
Daniel	604-535 BC
Zechariah	520-518 BC

The three Psalms were written by David under the inspiration of the Holy Spirit. David lived from 1041 BC to 971 BC.

As you read the Bible and encounter the prophecies, you will discover that all near-term prophecies have been fulfilled literally, and long-term prophecies have also been fulfilled literally. When you allow that revelation to sink in, you will begin to understand why you can trust the Bible and why you can expect that all the yet-to-be-fulfilled long-term prophecies will also be fulfilled literally. The fulfillment of the prophecies, especially the hundreds of Messianic prophecies, the miracles and signs that Jesus performed while He walked on earth ... *these have been written in order that you may believe that Jesus is the Messiah, the Son of God, and that through your faith in him you may have life. (John 20:31)*

11

Final chapter

Find out for yourself how good the Lord is. (Psalm 34:8)

Find out for yourself

Occasionally when someone asks me what I think about a topic (usually a controversial topic about which they have already made up their mind), I begin my answer by first asking, "Do you use a computer at work or at home?" The answer is invariably, "Yes." I then remind them that the speed at which computers execute instructions and do computations is measured in nanoseconds. A nanosecond is 1 billionth of a second! I then state, "You should not spend one nanosecond wondering or asking me what I think about that topic. You should instead find out for yourself what God says about the topic. If you're not sure where to find that information in the Bible, I'll be glad to help you. If you don't want to take the time to find out for yourself, I'll be glad to share what the Bible says about that topic and it will be up to you to check the scriptures to determine if what I am telling you is the truth." *(Acts 17:11)*

Best Sellers List

What book are you currently reading? Has it made its way to any of the best seller lists? Did you know that the Bible is the #1 book in the list of world-wide best sellers? Any search of the Internet will reveal that over 5 (some say 6) billion copies have been sold. The number of copies sold for the #2 book, Quotations from Chairman Mao Tse-Tung, is 900 million. The Bible is ahead by 4 or 5 billion copies. The cynic might ask, "If the Bible is the #1 best-selling book in the world, why isn't the world a better place?" It's a fair question. Here are several possible reasons:

1. People are purchasing Bibles but are not taking the time to read them.
2. People start reading the Bible but stop because of unfamiliar words like begat or strange names of people and places.
3. People start reading the Bible but stop when they encounter something with which they disagree.
4. People start reading the Bible but the style of writing doesn't appeal to them so it doesn't hold their interest and/or they find it boring.
5. People read the Bible but they don't put it into practice.

I believe #5 is the most significant reason the world isn't a better place. The following verse is a good example of God having our best interest in mind. *Do not deceive yourselves by just listening to God's word, instead, put it into practice. (James 1:22)*

It's not enough to go to church for one hour on Sunday to hear a sermon or listen to a Christian radio station during your drive-time, or listen to a preacher on TV, or attend a weekly Bible study, or listen to a Bible study on tape or CD or I-Pod. If you want to experience the best that God has in mind for you, you must put what you read into practice.

How much better would the world be if people put the following into practice:

> *Love your enemies, bless those who curse you,*
> *do good to those who hate you and pray for*
> *those who spitefully use you and persecute you.*
> *(Luke 6:27-28)*

Abraham Lincoln, who reportedly read the Bible three times before the age of 12, understood the importance of putting God's words into practice. A colleague of Lincoln's once asked him, "Why didn't you destroy your adversary while you had the chance?" Lincoln replied, "If I make an enemy a friend, haven't I destroyed an enemy?" (www.goodreads. com/quotes Abraham Lincoln)

One final observation: For those who do take the time to read the Bible and put it into practice, their world is a better place from their perspective.

The Age of Enlightenment

In conclusion, you may think I'm just one more person who looked into this Christianity thing, checked my mind at the door, and am living back in the Dark Ages, ignoring all that has been revealed by science, technology, philosophy, etc. since the Age of Enlightenment. According to Kant, the Enlightenment was "Mankind's final coming of age, the emancipation of the human consciousness from an immature state of ignorance and error." (Wikipedia (Kant))

Make no mistake: The Age of Enlightenment began when God stepped into humanity in the person of Jesus of Nazareth.

I think that's a good note to end on.

Printed in the United States
By Bookmasters